why we love
MOMS

Kids on Milk and Cookies,
Hugs and Kisses, and Other
Great Things About Mom

Angela Smith &
Jennifer Sander

Adams Media
Avon, Massachusetts

Published by Adams Media, an F+W Publications Company
57 Littlefield Street, Avon, MA 02322. U.S.A.
www.adamsmedia.com

ISBN 10: 1-59337-733-9
ISBN 13: 978-1-59337-733-5

Printed in Canada.

J I H G F E D C B A

Library of Congress Cataloging-in-Publication Data
Smith, Angela.
Why we love moms / Angela Smith and Jennifer Sander.
p. cm.
ISBN-13: 978-1-59337-733-5
ISBN-10: 1-59337-733-9
1. Mothers—Quotations. 2. Children—Quotations. I. Sander, Jennifer Basye. II. Title.
PN6084.M6S65 2007
818'.60208092052—dc22

2006102178

This publication is designed to provide accurate and authoritative information with regard to the subject matter covered. It is sold with the understanding that the publisher is not engaged in rendering legal, accounting, or other professional advice. If legal advice or other expert assistance is required, the services of a competent professional person should be sought.
—From a *Declaration of Principles* jointly adopted by a Committee of the American Bar Association and a Committee of Publishers and Associations

Many of the designations used by manufacturers and sellers to distinguish their product are claimed as trademarks. Where those designations appear in this book and Adams Media was aware of a trademark claim, the designations have been printed with initial capital letters.

This book is available at quantity discounts for bulk purchases.
For information, please call 1-800-289-0963.

contents

introduction

I have spent many years around young children. My first job was babysitting my three younger cousins. While attending college I worked at a preschool. Finally, I ended up teaching kindergarten while raising my own two sons.

One thing I've noticed through all my years spending time with young children . . . they just say the cutest things. They are so honest, innocent, and impulsive. Be careful, a five-year-old will tell you exactly what he is thinking if you ask.

I hope you enjoy this brief peek into the mind of a kindergartner as you hear how they truly view their parents. Some of the answers will make you smile in recognition, some of them will make you laugh, and some are heartbreaking in their honest emotion.

—*Angela Smith*

i love my mom because...

Why do young children love their moms? As parents, we might assume their reasons are emotional—because we protect them, because we nurture them. Surprise! Who knew that, according to children, it is because "she reads me Dr. Seuss books," or "she gets me root beer candy"? Children are far more practical and clear-eyed than we imagine—keep that root beer candy coming!

i love my mom because...

She helps me clean my room.

Joey, age 6

She's my favorite mom in the whole wide world.

Kelan, age 5

She's always there for me.

Cassie, age 5½

**She's my mom and
she loves me.**

Claire, age 5

i love my mom because...

She is really calm. She doesn't get stressed out.

Natalie, age 5

She just loves me and she's supposed to— 'cause she's my mom!

Declan, age 5

4

We are a family.

Rachel, age 5

Because she washes the clothes for me.

Isabella, age 6

She gives kisses and hugs . . . little kisses and big hugs.

Dalten, age 5

She loves me too.

Amber, age 5

She is special and nice.

Amanda, age 5

She's my mom.

Jacob, age 5

She feeds me and she's the "specialist" mom!

Morgan, age 5

She's funny and she's cool!

Julia, age 5

She's my friend too!

Michael, age 5

I just do.

Brennen, age 6

i love my mom because…

She makes yummy stuff sometimes.

Sterling, age 5

She helps me with lots of stuff.

Morgan, age 6

i love my mom because...

She's the best
mom ever.

Dodger, age 6

**She likes to play games
with me.**

Ashley, age 6

She makes a lotta good cookies!
(said with a huge smile)

Mabelita, age 5

She makes my favorite food for me . . . pizza!

Garret, age 5

I like to play with her.

Max, age 6

She stops my brother from hitting me.

Jonathan, age 7

She makes good cakes.

Marko, age 5

She plays Candyland with me.

Grace, age 5

She's so happy.

Rachel, age 5

She reads me
Dr. Seuss books.

Zoe, age 5

**She gets me
really cool stuff.**

Hunter, age 6

i love my mom because...

All kids love their mom, you're supposed to.

Megan, age 6

**She loves me and
I love her back.**

Jamie, age 5

She cuddles with
me in bed.

Michael, age 7

She lets us buy stuff at the store.

Scott, age 7

She really is nice to me.

Pierce, age 7

i love my mom because...

She snuggles with me.

Carter, age 6

She cooks me
good dinners.

Rose, age 7

She takes good
care of me.

Brooke, age 6

She cooks dinner.

Garret, age 6

She lets me sleep in her bed and watch movies at 9:00.

James, age 7

She's funny.

Samantha, age 6

She always has fun with me.

Zoey, age 7

She's kind to me.

Cade, age 5

She's not a mean mom— EVER!

Grant, age 8

She really likes me 'cause
I do good stuff.

Max, age 5

She be's nice to me.

Sterling, age 5

i love my mom because...

She likes to swim with me.

Lillieth, age 5

I get to help her shop at the store.

Kylie, age 5

i love my mom because...

She gets up early out
of bed if I want something
like my Star Wars toys.

Colin, age 6

She buys me licorice.

Summer, age 6

She hugs me every day.

Brandon, age 6

**She tucks me
into bed.**

Toby, age 5

She gets me rootbeer candy, and I really liked it. It was in her car.

Matthew, age 6

She helps me with my reading homework. Chapter books are kind of hard.

Garrett, age 6

She helps me make lunch.

Rebecca, age 7

She is kind, pretty, and nice.

Lane, age 8

i need my mom because...

Think of a child's basic needs—warmth, shelter, food. Add some of the reasons our respondents need their mommies—snickerdoodles and chocolate chip pancakes with chocolate syrup. It is clear to one girl why she needs her mother, because "without my mom I wouldn't be here." A good point she makes there, as obvious as the girl who pointed out that she needs her mother because "I can't babysit myself." Oh.

**She drives us to school
or to anywhere.**

Joey, age 6

She gives me grape
flavored medicine when
I'm cough sick.

Kelan, age 5

She starts my motorcycle.
I don't know how to.

Will, age 5

We play cards.

Cassie, age 5½

She gives me what I want for my birthday.

Claire, age 5

She watches over me while my dad works.

Natalie, age 5

She can keep me safe.

Declan, age 5

She drives me somewhere.

isabella, age 6

She feeds me sugared oatmeal. It's my favorite!

Dalten, age 5

Because I get hurt sometimes.

Amber, age 5

i need my mom because...

She makes me dinner a lot.

Brandon, age 6

So I can live.

Garret, age 5

She makes me dinner.
She makes me lunch.
She takes me places
and to McDonalds and
Burger King.

Jacob, age 5

I might get sick.

Morgan, age 5

She takes care of me.

Carson, age 6

She makes me happy.
She tickles me.

Julia, age 5

She sings lullabies to me.

Michael, age 5

I'm good with her.

Bennen, age 6

She snuggles with me before i go to bed.

Parker, age 6

i need my mom because...

Some stuff is hard and she helps me.

Sterling, age 5

She feeds me and plays with me.

Morgan, age 6

She helps us work and stuff.

Dodger, age 6

She helps me do stuff I can't and spell words. She's a good speller.

Ashley, age 6

She helps me to sew a lot. She's famous 'cause she knows how to sew a lot of hard things.

Mabelita, age 5

She helps with
homework
if I don't know how
to do the new stuff.

Garret, age 5

i love her.

Trenton, age 6

She helps me with my words.

Marko, age 5

She's a great mom.

Grace, age 5

She helps me do the stuff
I don't like to do.

Rachel, age 5

So she can give loves.

Zoe, age 5

i love her. You need to have people to love.

Hunter, age 6

She makes the best breakfasts like chocolate chip pancakes with chocolate syrup.

Megan, age 6

i need my mom because...

She helps me learn things.

Jamie, age 5

She cooks good food for me.

Anna, age 5

Without my mom
I wouldn't be here.

Michael, age 7

**She takes me
to school.**

Scott, age 7

if i didn't have her, who would do the dishes? My dad couldn't— 'cuz he's at work. i couldn't do them —'cuz i'd break them.

Pierce, age 7

She gets my clothes out and makes me snickerdoodles.

Carter, age 6

She always loves on me.

Rose, age 7

**She does good
stuff for me.**

Brooke, age 6

If she wasn't alive I
wouldn't even be here.

James, age 7

She tells me to clean my room—my dad doesn't do it. It wouldn't get clean.

Samantha, age 6

When i get hurt she helps me.

Zoey, age 7

To help me when I fight with my sister.

Cade, age 5

When I broke my leg on my dirt bike she took care of me.

Grant, age 8

She likes to go to the mall
with me and my family
except my dad. He doesn't
like the mall.

Lillieth, age 5

I get boo-boos sometimes!

Sterling, age 5

If I fall down she can help me up.

Kylie, age 5

She likes to tickle me. i really like that.

Sophia, age 5

I can't babysit myself.
I'm too little.

Summer, age 6

Without her I wouldn't have been born.

Hannah, age 6

If I didn't have her I wouldn't have any food. My dad can't cook.

Colin, age 6

She cleans the house.
If she wasn't there we'd
have dirt all over and
then the insects and
reptiles would come in.

Garrett, age 6

She gives me pushes on my bike.

Matthew, age 6

She can buy stuff for me.

Forest, age 7

i need my mom because she needs me.

Sarah, age 7

the funniest thing about my mom is...

Pratfalls and funny faces score big with the kindergarten set, as do some parental attempts at singing, and a few foibles in the kitchen. We should all heed the advice of one young man and not cook with beets. Why? "The food turns pink." Some moms aren't funny at all, though, according to one expert observer—"I think I missed all the funny things she does." Hope she keeps watching!

She dressed up as a Blues Brother for Halloween. That's a brother that dresses in the same clothes.

Kelan, age 6

When she says funny things.

Joey, age 6

She does funny dances— she goes in circles.

Will, age 5

When she laughs at me.

Cassie, age 5½

Her funny faces.
She looks like a tiger.

Claire, age 5

She makes funny breakfasts like Minnie Mouse pancakes with a funny face.

Natalie, age 5

She makes me laugh.

Rachel, age 5

67

the funniest thing about my mom is...

She plays with me.

Isabella, age 6

She can scare me . . .
she jumps off something
to scare me and make
me laugh. I love it when
she does this.

Dalten, age 5

She tickles me.

Brandon, age 6

She shows me funny tricks and funny faces. My favorite face is the monkey face.

Amanda, age 5

the funniest thing about my mom is...

That she tells jokes.

Jacob, age 5

She embarrasses us.

Morgan, age 5

She sings in the car.
She sings bad.

Carson, age 6

She has a great laugh.

Julia, age 5

When she tickles my
face with a feather
I found.

Michael, age 5

**She hurts herself when
she's combing her hair.
She brushes too hard
and gets hurt.**

Brennen, age 6

She dances with me and my brother.

Parker, age 6

When she's telling jokes—
except for my dad.
He's funnier.

Sterling, age 5

When she tries to get bones from my dog. She looks funny.

Morgan, age 6

She laughs a lot.

Dodger, age 6

Sometimes she makes a mistake while cooking and puts funny things in our food. Then my daddy won't like it.

Mabelita, age 5

She cooks food with beets in them. The food turns PINK!

Garret, age 5

That she always laughs at me.

Trenton, age 6

She sings funny.

Max, age 6

When she spills eggs everywhere. Yellow was everywhere in the refrigerator.

Marko, age 5

She can make funny sounds.

Rachel, age 5

She works two jobs.
Three jobs—she also
takes care of me
and Zackery.

Zoe, age 5

I think I missed all the
funny things she does.

Megan, age 6

**She likes to
stay in bed.**

Jamie, age 5

When I hurt my arm she always tells me she's going to buy me a new arm.

Anna, age 5

She sneaks peeks of pictures of me when i was a baby.

Michael, age 7

80

She's afraid of alligator lizards.

Scott, age 7

She teaches at my school.

Carter, age 6

She repeats every word she says.

James, age 7

She races me on
my bike.

Cade, age 5

She makes up real good jokes about us.

Grant, age 8

She likes to watch the joke show.

Sterling, age 5

She likes to have fun and go to college and pick flowers.

Lillieth, age 5

She laughs all the time when people talk to her.

Kylie, age 5

the funniest thing about my mom is...

She makes chicken pancakes. They look like chickens.

Sophia, age 5

She likes to give me tickles on my tummy.

Summer, age 6

She likes to sleep on me
and use me as a pillow.

Brandon, age 6

**She makes up songs
about barbecued
steaks.**

Toby, age 5

She does criss cross applesauce and she's all grown up! Only kindergartners are suppose to sit that way.

Hannah, age 6

When she plays with my little brother she talks like a baby.

Garrett, age 6

She bear hugs me and cracks my back.

Darlene, age 6

Her thighs are big.

Robert, age 8

She forgets.
All the time.

Kevin, age 7

She acts crazy in the car to music.

Sarah, age 7

when i am a mom i will...

So how will the little girls we talked to do it differently when years from now it is their turn to be a mom? Some girls have big career plans in the works—"I'll be a movie star and my kids will go to the babysitter." Others are already hard at work planning future meals—"I'll take my kids out for ice cream and have lunch with them." We're guessing she already knows what kind of ice cream she will order too!

Read my kids books.

Cassie, age 5½

Stay at home and play with my three kids.

Claire, age 5

Take care of my kids.

Natalie, age 5

Have babies.

Rachel, age 5

Play games.

Isabella, age 6

Take my kids to the water park.

Dalten, age 5

Take care of babies.

Amber, age 5

Protect my children from "bad guys" and save them.

Amanda, age 5

when i am a mom i will...

Go to the park.

Jacob, age 5

I won't be a mom,
I'll be a dad.

Carson, age 6

Take my kids to the park and on picnics.

Morgan, age 6

I'll be a movie star and my kids will go to the babysitter.

Ashley, age 6

I won't be a mom because I don't want to get any babies. I'll miss my mom and dad too much to get married.

Mabelita, age 5

Drive to the Spaghetti Factory!

Rachel, age 5

Have fun with my kids.

Zoe, age 5

Talk on the phone.

Jamie, age 5

Clean my kids' room.

Anna, age 5

Tell my kids to clean up after themselves.

Samantha, age 6

i'll take my kids out to ice cream and have lunch with them.

Zoey, age 7

Still go see my dad whenever i have time to go.

Ashley, age 6

Work at Starbucks! Because my daddy loves Starbucks!

Grace, age 5

when i am a mom i will...

Fix a garden.

Mabelita, age 5

Help the dad.

Zoe, age 5

Clean my room.

isabella, age 6

Pick flowers for my mom
when she is old and go
to the park with her.

Lillieth, age 5

Go to the mall and shop everyday!

Sophia, age 5

Have one baby.
Only a girl baby.

Summer, age 6

Be a vet and help animals. I'm also going to have girl triplets. Their names will be Jennifer, Crystal, and Rose.

Hannah, age 6

Do my kid's hair.

Darlene, age 6

Try to keep my kids healthy.

Giovana, age 7

Work! I'm gonna be a firewoman!

Hannah, age 6

i'm happiest when mom...

How can you keep a child happy? Sure, toys are always a safe bet, but simple things like "a surprise of cookies," or bowling together or eating dinner at home will also do the trick. Praying together, reading together, eating together, playing together, you can see the theme emerging here . . . Oh, and kids are also happiest when they are not in "time-out." Who would have guessed!

Makes us pizza.

Joey, age 6

Gives me bandages and medicine.

Kelan, age 5

Cleans my Hot Wheels area. It really gets messy.

Will, age 5

Tickles me.

Claire, age 5

Plays with me on my trampoline.

Natalie, age 5

Draws me pictures.
She likes to draw me
pictures of a heart.

Declan, age 5

Helps me with my homework.

Rachel, age 5

Does a lot of things like reading books.

Isabella, age 6

**Says prayers with me.
We pray for Jesus.**

Dalten, age 5

Does fun things like
playing tag.

Brandon, age 6

Plays games with me. She likes to trick me. She hides and scares me.

Amanda, age 5

When she takes me out to places.

Jacob, age 5

i'm happiest when mom...

She snuggles with me.

Morgan, age 5

Tucks me in bed.

Carson, age 6

Plays tag with me.

Julia, age 5

Makes a mask out of a box and puts it on my head. She cuts out eyeholes and mouth holes.

Michael, age 5

i'm happiest when mom...

Be's nice to me.

Brennen, age 6

Lets my dog sleep
in my room.

Parker, age 6

Plays with me.

Sterling, age 5

Makes me laugh.

Dodger, age 6

i'm happiest when mom...

Makes surprises for me.

Mabelita, age 5

Lets me play backyard
baseball on the computer.

Garret, age 5

120

i'm happiest when mom...

Takes me to get toys like Power Rangers.

Trenton, age 6

Plays computer with me.

Max, age 6

Makes me cakes.

Marko, age 5

Makes chocolate chip
and oatmeal cookies at
night when I'm asleep.
I get a surprise of
cookies in the morning.

Grace, age 5

Kisses me.

Rachel, age 5

Sleeps with me.

Zoe, age 5

i'm happiest when mom...

Hugs me.

Hunter, age 6

Doesn't put me in time-out.

Megan, age 6

i'm happiest when mom...

Stays home and watches movies with me.

Jamie, age 5

Lets me sleep in her bed for the whole night!

Anna, age 5

Hugs me and kisses me.

Michael, age 7

Has bowling night with me.

Pierce, age 7

Kisses and snuggles me.

Carter, age 6

Lets me eat candy! And she sometimes does.

Jonathan, age 7

Takes me to school.

Rose, age 7

Lets me have fast food.

Garret, age 6

Takes me to the bowling alley.

James, age 7

Plays soccer with me. She's good.

Grant, age 8

Gets me food at her work like applesauce.

Kylie, age 5

Sends my brother to get some ice cream—vanilla, my favorite.

Summer, age 6

Eats at home. When we eat pasta or maybe Chinese. Mom's favorite is orange chicken.

Hannah, age 6

Goes to the store to buy fruit. Watermelon is my favorite. i like the seeds.

Colin, age 6

Prays with me at night.
We pray about toys.

Toby, age 5

Gets out my clothes in
the morning and makes
my bed.

Garrett, age 6

Reads books to me at night.

Kevin, age 7

She pulls up my covers and kisses me goodnight.

Sarah, age 7

Plays Snood on the computer with me.

Samantha, age 6

Makes my bed in the morning.

Cade, age 5

i'm saddest when my mom...

Children told us they are often sad when something happens to them, and are equally sensitive when their mother is the one who is sad. No one likes to be spanked, or yelled at, or left behind when their mommy goes to work, but we were surprised by their sweet concern for mothers who are tired, hurt, or have a headache.

Doesn't listen to me.

Joey, age 6

Isn't here.

Kelan, age 5

Doesn't help me clean my Hot Wheels.

Will, age 5

Leaves, 'cause I miss her. I have to stay with a babysitter.

Cassie, age 5½

Goes on vacations without me, because i miss her a lot.

Claire, age 5

Leaves for a meeting because I always miss her 'cause she's the best in the family.

Natalie, age 5

Goes to work, because I love her and miss her.

Declan, age 5

Be's mad at me.

Isabella, age 6

Gets her toenail removed. She had to go to the doctor to get her toenail taken off.

Dalten, age 5

Goes away.

Amber, age 5

140

Spanks my butt.

Brandon, age 6

Gets hurt.

Amanda, age 5

Has a headache.

Carson, age 6

Is tired, but then I give
her a bear . . .
she likes bears.

Michael, age 5

Won't give me ice cream.

Parker, age 6

Yells at me because it hurts my ears.

Sterling, age 5

Goes to Bible study
at night.

Morgan, age 6

**Gets mad when I do
wrong things I'm not
suppose to do.**

Ashley, age 6

i'm saddest when my mom...

Leaves.

Mabelita, age 5

Yells at me
when I don't listen.

Garret, age 5

Doesn't take me out to dinner.

Trenton, age 6

Talks only to my brother.

Jonathan, age 7

Yells at me because I do something wrong.

Max, age 6

Forgets to tell me that she is proud of me.

Marko, age 5

Goes out to feed the horses without me. i love to feed the horses.

Grace, age 5

Spanks me—I cry!
If I do it on purpose—
I get a spank.

Rachel, age 5

Goes to work, because she comes home too late. 8:00!

Zoe, age 5

Trips. One time I accidentally tripped her.

Hunter, age 6

Puts me in time-out.

Megan, age 6

Lets my older sister help me babysit my little brother—he's one.

Anna, age 5

i'm saddest when my mom...

Leaves for San Diego.

Scott, age 7

Has to go on a trip.

Pierce, age 7

i'm saddest when my mom...

Leaves me for work.

Rose, age 7

Doesn't make dinner.

Garret, age 6

i'm saddest when my mom...

Grounds me.

James, age 7

Cries.

Samantha, age 6

i'm saddest when my mom...

Is away from me.

Zoey, age 7

Spanks my bottom even though i'm a turd.

Cade, age 5

Works on our apartments.

Grant, age 8

Forgets to pack my lunch and I starve to death.

Max, age 5

Gets mad if i don't clean my room.

Sterling, age 5

Won't play outside after it rains.

Lillieth, age 5

Gets me in trouble if I hurt somebody.

Kylie, age 5

Is home by herself when my dad is gone at school.

Sophia, age 5

Makes me have a time-out with spankings.

Summer, age 6

Goes bye-bye to places i don't know about.

Brandon, age 6

Goes an' be's a dental assistant. She works in people's mouths and I miss her when she is there.

Hannah, age 6

Puts me in my room for two seconds because I was naughty.

Colin, age 6

Gets hurt and breaks her toenails. It scares her.

Matthew, age 6

Puts me in time-out
for bothering my little
brother. I just wanted him
to wake up from his nap
so we could play.

Garrett, age 6

Argues with me about eating dinner.

Toby, age 5

Is a grumbler.

Eladio, age 6

Gets mad at me when I slam the door.

Darlene, age 6

Doesn't talk to me.

Rebecca, age 7

i'm saddest when my mom...

Leaves to go to
a friend's house.

Forest, age 7

the best thing my mom can do is...

All children believe their mom is the best. Some are the best in the kitchen (Bacon! Spaghetti! Macaroni and cheese!), others are champion TV-watchers, or prize-winning scrapbookers. And what mom wouldn't be proud that her child has noticed his mom's first rate skill at running the dishwasher—"she's good at putting the knives in so she doesn't get cut." Keep up the great work, ladies!

Brush horses and shave them with clippers.

Joey, age 6

Artwork. She's good at just the regular artwork stuff.

Kelan, age 5

Ride her quad good!

Will, age 5

She can cook because my grandpa is a cook.

Cassie, age 5½

Cook. She's a great cook. My favorite is Chinese.

Claire, age 5

Jump really high . . . well, she used to jump as high as her head.

Natalie, age 5

Play soccer . . .
she kicks the ball and
is the fastest runner.

Declan, age 5

Feed us.

Rachael, age 5

Take me to the doctor when my cheeks hurt . . . She knows sleeping makes my cheeks feel better.

Dalten, age 5

Work at her post office.

Amber, age 5

Build houses.

Brandon, age 6

Read *Sunset* magazine
for yard ideas. She has
the best yard.

Amanda, age 5

She takes stuff down
when I need it.

Jacob, age 5

**Work at home.
Actually she's good
at everything good.**

Morgan, age 5

the best thing my mom can do is...

Watch *That's So Raven* with me.

Julia, age 5

Cook Cheerios for me.

Michael, age 5

173

the best thing my mom can do is...

Go to the gym.

Brennen, age 6

Help with my homework.

Parker, age 6

Cook dinner.

Sterling, age 5

Cook macaroni.

Dodger, age 6

the best thing my mom can do is...

Make pancakes.

Ashley, age 6

Take care of my daddy.

Mabelita, age 5

the best thing my mom can do is...

Work out.

Garret, age 5

Make shell pasta with cheese.

Trenton, age 6

the best thing my mom can do is...

Make pasta—plain pasta with salt.

Max, age 6

Make the best cakes and brownies.

Marko, age 5

Go outside and play
with me—when my
sister is at school.

Grace, age 5

Make heart flowers
for me.

Rachel, age 5

Take me to Disneyland because i love Splash Mountain.

Zoe, age 5

Make macaroni & cheese.

Hunter, age 6

Get my birthday party ready.

Megan, age 6

Watch the sunset with me.

Jamie, age 5

Cook Hawaii pizza with pineapples!

Anna, age 5

Make stuff from India with curry sauce.

Michael, age 7

Let me have friends over.

Scott, age 7

Be nice to me.

Pierce, age 7

the best thing my mom can do is...

Make snickerdoodles.

Carter, age 6

Cook salad.

Rose, age 7

the best thing my mom can do is...

Draw a cat.

Brooke, age 6

Do laundry.

Garret, age 6

Have me as her son.

James, age 7

Act weird.

Zoey, age 7

Clean my room.

Cade, age 5

Hug me really hard. She hugs me hard but doesn't squeeze my guts out.

Max, age 5

Make chicken nuggets.
She can even make them
just like McDonald's.
She has the secret recipe.
She's magic.

Sterling, age 5

Take me shopping to Target. They have lots of toys there.

Kylie, age 5

Kill spiders. She's the best at it.

Sophia, age 5

Tell me we are going to Disneyland really soon.

Summer, age 6

Test my sister with her karate.

Brandon, age 6

Jump on a trampoline. She can do a double flip and she's old—31!

Hannah, age 6

Buy me a snake. The python kind. My brother used to have one but he lost it upstairs.

Colin, age 6

Take me to the zoo to see the giraffes. I love their spots and they are very tall.

Toby, age 5

Cook Spaghetti-Os. They are my favorite. They come in a can.

Matthew, age 6

Run the dishwasher. She's good at putting the knives in so she doesn't get cut. They're very sharp!

Garrett, age 6

Cook bacon.

Darlene, age 6

Make me a great lunch.

Rebecca, age 7

Scrapbooking is what my mom does best.

Brittany, age 6½

my mom looks
silly when she...

Words to the wise, mothers. If you don't want your children to giggle at you don't ever salsa dance, dress up like a mummy for a costume party, put on a hat of any kind, or try to look like Zorro's girlfriend. Oh, and keep that bumblebee costume in the closet, please.

Tells funny stories.

Joey, age 6

Dresses up.

Kelan, age 5

Dances.

Will, age 5

Puts wigs on.

Cassie, age 5½

Does the salsa dance.
She looks really funny.
She twirls around.

Claire, age 5

**Dresses up as a
mummy with bandages.**

Natalie, age 5

my mom looks silly when she...

Makes faces.

Declan, age 5

Plays with me.

Isabella, age 6

Makes a crazy face . . . she looks like a crazy man.

Dalten, age 5

Looks out the window to watch us play.

Amber, age 5

my mom looks silly when she...

Makes a monkey face.

Amanda, age 5

She wears silly hats.

Morgan, age 5

Takes me to school because she just gets out of bed.

Carson, age 6

**Sings in the car.
She looks funny.**

Julia, age 5

Makes funny eyes at me.

Michael, age 5

Drops her workout weights on the carpet.

Brennen, age 6

Plays peek-a-boo with me.

Morgan, age 6

Puts colored pens on her head and walks without them falling out.

Mabelita, age 5

Puts a hat on.

Dodger, age 6

Plugs her nose and chases us.

Ashley, age 6

Dresses up. Once she tried to be Zorro's girlfriend. She changed her mind 'cuz none of the stuff fitted and so she was a pirate.

Garret, age 5

my mom looks silly when she...

Jumps off the bed and flies down.

Trenton, age 6

Works out.

Max, age 6

Drops things and says "UH OH"!

Marko, age 5

Sits on my dad's lap— 'cuz she looks too big for his lap.

Zoe, age 5

my mom looks silly when she...

Gets up in the morning and her hair is sticking up.

Jamie, age 5

Does a funny face.

Michael, age 7

Sticks her tongue out.

Scott, age 7

Is doing funny things—
just being funny.

Pierce, age 7

Takes her glasses off.

Rose, age 7

Wears funny outfits. She looks funny but she thinks it looks really good.

Sophia, age 5

Does crazy stuff.

Brooke, age 6

Tries to speak French.

Jonathan, age 7

Gets her picture taken. She looks funny in pictures.

Grant, age 8

Wears a funny hair thing on her head. It looks funny, like part of a mask. It's supposed to make her hair look pretty.

Kylie, age 5

Tries out karate moves.

Brandon, age 6

Dances. She does the kind of dance where you put your dress up in the air.

Colin, age 6

215

Twists up her legs and does pretzels with her legs. She can even walk like that. She looks like she could be in a circus.

Hannah, age 6

Puts her fingers in her mouth.

Matthew, age 6

Wiggles around.

Rebecca, age 7

Dresses up in a bumblebee outfit. I don't know why she does it. She just likes doing it.

Garrett, age 6

Mostly she looks silly when she sleeps.

Jonathan, age 7

My mom looks silly even when she isn't silly.

Sarah, age 7

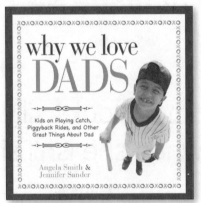